MAY TH

THIS BOOK INSPIRE YOU
AND BRING YOU COMFORT.

GOD BLESS,
ROGER KOBIE
2-9-12

WHAT TO DO WHEN YOUR WORLD IS FALLING APART

RICHARD EXLEY

13 12 11 10 09   10 9 8 7 6 5 4 3 2 1

What To Do When Your World Is Falling Apart
ISBN 13: 978-0-9842534-6-3
ISBN 10: 0-9842534-6-7
Copyright © 2009 by Richard Exley

Published by Vallew Press
P.O. Box 54744
Tulsa, OK 74155

Distributed by Word and Spirit Resources
P.O. Box 701403
Tulsa, OK 74170

For my sister

Cheryl Lavonne Exley Echols,

known to her many friends as Sherry,

and affectionately to her three brothers

as "Tots."

Your faith and your courage

are an inspiration

to everyone who knows you.

You are our heroine

and we love you.

TABLE OF CONTENTS

CHAPTER 1

THE PERFECT STORM

"Before very long, a wind of hurricane force, called the 'northeaster,' swept down from the island. The ship was caught by the storm and could not head into the wind; so we gave way to it and were driven along. ...When neither sun nor stars appeared for many days and the storm continued raging, we finally gave up all hope of being saved. After the men had gone a long time without food, Paul stood up before them and said: '...I urge you to keep up your courage, because not one of you will be lost; only the ship will be destroyed. Last night an angel of the God whose I am and whom I serve stood beside me and said, 'Do not be afraid, Paul. You must stand trial before Caesar; and God has graciously given you the lives of all who sail with you.' So keep up your courage, men, for I have faith in God that it will happen just as he told me."

ACTS 27:14,15,20-25

THE PERFECT STORM

~~~~~~~~~

I've lived long enough to know that if I'm not right in the middle of a storm, then I'm probably just coming out of one; and if I'm not just coming out of a storm, then I'm probably just about to go into one. That's not a negative confession, it's biblical truth! Job 5:7 declares, "…man is born to trouble as surely as sparks fly upward." And Jesus himself said, "In this world you will have trouble. But take heart! I have overcome the world" (John 16:33).

In this passage Jesus gives us two important truths. First, He tells us that trouble is inevitable. It's coming—there's no way to escape it. Pretending nothing bad will ever happen to you is not only naïve, but foolish. Both Scripture and history reveal that the storms of life come against the righteous and the unrighteous alike. In this world you are going to have trouble no matter how much faith you have, so prepare for it.

In recent months the world as we know it has been shaken. Things many of us thought were unshakable have collapsed. There have been bank failures and government bailouts; the housing market has imploded; the stock market has plunged; many of us have lost nearly half of our 401K's; the Federal Government is running General Motors; unemployment is at a twenty-five year high. Federal spending is completely out of control and our nation is plunging towards bankruptcy. If things continue this way our children and grandchildren will be saddled with a federal debt that is unimaginable.

If you haven't been affected yet, you will. I'm not trying to scare you, but I want to prepare you for the coming storm. No one goes through life unscathed— no one. In time, you will face things that will rock your world. Your storm may come in any number of different ways. You may find yourself suddenly unemployed with no way to provide for your family or make the mortgage payment; you may discover that your fifteen-year-old daughter has had an abortion and you didn't even know she was pregnant; your husband of twenty-seven years may inform you that he is in love with a younger woman and that he wants a divorce; you may give birth to a severely handicapped child or your precious grandson may be diagnosed with Leukemia; a drunk driver may kill your seventeen-year-old son on his way home from a football game. These are not imaginary scenarios, but real-life situations that I have encountered as a pastor.

"In this world you will have trouble…" (John 16:33).

Lest you think I'm exaggerating, let me share a random sampling of the storms my friends and acquaintances have battled in recent weeks.

A pastoral colleague telephoned me when a gut-wrenching tragedy rocked his world. Between sobs he told me that a husband and wife, both members of his congregation, had been arguing when things got out of hand. In a fit of temper the husband grabbed a pistol and shot his wife twice, killing her. "I can't believe it," he sobbed. "These people weren't low-lifes. They were well respected in the church. The husband was like a son to me. Now he's in jail facing murder charges, his wife's body is in the morgue, and our church family is in shock."

"In this world you will have trouble…" (John 16:33).

Then there's the college president who suffered a massive heart attack at barely fifty years old. In an instant his world came crashing down. Subsequently, he underwent by-pass surgery and, while he was recovering, his father passed away. When he thought the worst was over, he discovered that it was just the calm in the eye of the storm. Returning from his father's funeral he was blindsided by a small but vocal group of faculty who were actively working to have him removed as president. Given his physical and emotional condition he chose to resign rather than fight them. In five short months he went from a healthy, highly respected college president, to a grieving ex-college president battling depression.

"In this world you will have trouble..." (John 16:33).

And he's not alone. Today, unemployment is rampant. I received an email from a friend telling me that he had been laid off due to the poor economy. Through no fault of his own, he suddenly found himself past fifty and unemployed. "How," he wanted to know, "am I going make my mortgage payment and provide for my family? What if I can't find another job?"

"In this world you will have trouble…" (John 16:33).

There's more. I received an email from a ministerial colleague with an urgent prayer request from a desperate pastor's wife. While vacationing, their teenage son swam into an unmarked clear Plexiglas wall in the hotel swimming pool and broke his neck. He was taken to a trauma one medical center where a neurosurgeon operated for five hours fusing bone taken from the boy's hip into his neck. He will have to wear a "halo" that will immobilize his head and neck for three months. While the prognosis is uncertain, after the surgery he was able to move his arms and his legs responded to pain caused by pin-pricks administered by the neurosurgeon.

Unfortunately, trouble is no stranger to this family. Their oldest child suffers from severe Spina bifida and has had over a hundred surgeries. They are painfully familiar with doctors and hospitals but that hardly makes it easier. The mother writes, "We are all just sick about what has happened. We have cried all day. We hate it, but we will trust God and we will stay faithful."

"In this world you will have trouble..." (John 16:33).

Nor have my wife, Brenda, and I been immune to trouble. During the past five years we have been hit with one thing after another. First, Brenda's father was diagnosed with colon Cancer and given less than a year to live. Six months later I was preaching his funeral. While Brenda was still reeling from her father's death, our thirty-four year old daughter, Leah, was diagnosed with Systemic Lupus. She soon found it impossible to leave the house or care for her husband and their two small children. Once more Brenda became the principal caregiver. For the next two years she spent a significant portion of her time living with Leah and her husband, Douglas, in Tulsa.

Then my father fell and broke his hip, an injury from which he never recovered, and three months later he passed away. Next, one of my closest friends was stricken with Cancer. After a two-year battle he succumbed and, once again, I found myself preaching a funeral. Finally, just before Christmas, my mother had a massive aneurysm. We drove through the night hoping to reach Houston before she died. For nine days we sat in the hospital by her side, but she never regained consciousness and finally left this world on Friday morning, December 19th. Three days later we had her funeral. And now my sister is battling Cancer.

"In this world you will have trouble..." (John 16:33).

Although medical science has made significant advances in recent years, a diagnosis of Cancer still has the power to overwhelm. Let the doctor's diagnosis include "stage three," and the level of fear ratchets up yet again. And should the prognosis include a life expectancy of less than two years, the effect can be absolutely devastating. That's what my sister is facing as I write this today. In an instant, her world went from safe and secure to one of fearful uncertainty and confusion.

So where does she go from here? What does she do now? She is going to get the best medical advice available before deciding on a course of treatment, but beyond that what can she do? For that matter, what can any of us do when our world is falling apart?

Which brings us to the second truth Jesus gives us in John 16:33. It is at least as important as the first truth, and probably more so. He tells us not to be afraid no matter how overwhelming the trouble seems. He is more than a match for whatever trouble life throws at you! "Take heart," He says, "I have overcome the world" (John 16:33). Grab hold of this truth and hang on to it. It's your lifeline!

My sister, Sherry, said when the doctor first informed her that the golf ball sized tumor was malignant, it was like being punched in the stomach.

But after a few days the shock seemed to fade a little, only to return with a vengeance when she was informed that it was an internal melanoma–an extremely rare and deadly form of Cancer. Still, the full impact of her situation didn't hit her until she went to the MD Anderson Cancer Treatment Center to meet with a team of surgeons and oncologists. There she was confronted with the ravages of Cancer and its treatments first hand. The hallways and waiting rooms were filled with patients of all ages, in all stages of sickness and death.

"I felt like I was walking through the valley of the shadow of death," she told me. "Fear took me by the throat and I could hardly breath. Clutching my Bible to my chest I began to pray and rebuke fear. Little by little the fear receded and as I sensed God's nearness, a peace settled over me."

As she related that experience to me, I was reminded of an incident from my childhood. When I was just a boy of eight or nine, we lived in a green house, situated beneath towering Elm trees, on Chestnut Street in Sterling, Colorado. Much to the chagrin of the town fathers, Sterling was in the midst of a crime wave. Every week another home was burglarized and the police had made no arrests. In fact, they seemed clueless.

One evening, just before bedtime, I overheard dad and mom discussing the latest burglary. Needless to say the situation was making them uncomfortable, as it was most families. Their concern (or fear) must have been contagious because when I went to bed I couldn't think of anything else and awoke shortly after midnight to see a man rummaging through my closet. I tried to scream but I couldn't make a sound. Terror squeezed my throat shut, rendering me mute. For thirty seconds, a minute, maybe more, I couldn't do anything. I lay there frozen with fear. Finally I managed a blood-curdling scream and my father came charging into my bedroom. Of course, the intruder vanished instantly and, after a time, dad managed to calm my fears and I was able to go back to sleep.

Some time later I awoke again and the intruder was back; in fact he was standing right beside my bed. I lay there trying not to breath, more afraid than I had ever been. Suddenly I lunged straight up in bed and screamed loud enough to wake the dead. In an instant dad burst into the room, baseball bat in hand. Again, the intruder disappeared.

Now that I'm older I realize that intruder was most likely just a figment of my overactive imagination, but you couldn't have convinced me of that then. In fact, after the second experience, I refused to be comforted. My father's exhortations fell on deaf ears. It didn't matter that he had checked all the doors and windows and found them securely locked; it made no difference that he had gone through the house room by room without finding anything amiss. My fears would not be calmed. Finally, he carried my younger brother into the master bedroom and put him into bed with my mother. Then he climbed into bed beside me, and when he did my fear fled!

What answers, assurances, and exhortations could not do, my father's presence did. He comforted me. As long as he was with me I had no fear. Isn't this what the Psalmist is talking about when he writes:

> "Even though I walk
> through the valley of the shadow
> of death,
> **I will fear no evil,**
> **for you are with me;**
> your rod and your staff,
> they comfort me."
>
> PSALM 23:4

Throughout her battle with Cancer my sister has demonstrated a remarkable courage, and her faith has never wavered, not even in the face of overwhelming odds. How, you may be wondering, is she able to do it? There is only one reason. She is able to face her uncertain future without succumbing to fear because Father God is with her, and His presence is a constant source of courage and strength. When God walks in, fear has to flee!

As I look back over the past five years and review the troubles our family has faced, I have to admit that it has been nearly overwhelming at times. Nevertheless, our faith remains strong. God is showing us how to live triumphantly in the midst of all kinds of adversity and I am constantly reminding myself that, "If God is for us, who can be against us?" (Rom. 8:31).

In my darkest hours the apostle Paul has been an inspiration to me. No one faced more trouble than he did, yet he declared "…I am convinced that neither death nor life, neither angels nor demons, neither the present nor the future, nor any powers, neither height nor depth, nor anything else in all creation, will be able to separate us for the love of God that is in Christ Jesus our Lord" (Rom. 8:38-39). And then he shouts into the teeth of the storm, "…in all these we are more than conquerors through him who loved us" (Rom. 8:37).

It doesn't matter what you're facing—financial adversity, problems with your children, marital difficulties, or health issues. Jesus knows what you're up against and He cares about you. What touches you touches Him, and He is able to deliver you. So take heart!

In the next four chapters I am going to use Jesus' experience in Gethsemane (see Matt. 26:36-46) as a model to show you what to do when your world is falling apart.

1) Ask for help.
2) Run to the Father.
3) Surrender to the Father's will.
4) Stand firm—keep trusting even when your circumstances don't seem to be changing.

Practice these disciplines and you will be an overcomer no matter what kind of trouble life throws at you.

PRAYER

Lord Jesus, You are our only hope and a very present help in the time of trouble. We do not put our confidence in the government, or in the financial institutions of our nation, or even in medical science. Our confidence is in You and You alone. Grant us courage in the time of trouble and strength for the storm. In Your holy name we pray. Amen.

CHAPTER 2

A CORD OF
THREE STRANDS

"For when we came into Macedonia, this body of ours had no rest, but we were harassed at every turn—conflicts on the outside, fears within. But God, who comforts the downcast, comforted us by the coming of Titus, and not only by his coming but also by the comfort you had given him. He told us about your longing for me, your deep sorrow, your ardent concern for me, so that my joy was greater than ever. ...In addition to our own encouragement, we were especially delighted to see how happy Titus was, because his spirit has been refreshed by all of you."

2 CORINTHIANS 7:5-7,13

CHAPTER 2

A CORD OF THREE STRANDS

⎯⎯∞∞∞⎯⎯

I don't suppose any of us have ever faced a greater challenge than the one Jesus faced that final night in Gethsemane. From a human perspective His world was falling apart. Judas had already struck an agreement with the religious leaders to betray Him. Before the night was done Peter would deny Him three times and the rest of the disciples would desert Him.

He would be falsely accused and unjustly condemned by the Sanhedrin. The Roman Governor would have Him flogged before sentencing Him to death by crucifixion. And finally, as He was dying, God would turn His back on Him. (see Matt. 27:45, 46.)

So what did Jesus do when His world was falling apart?

The first thing He did was to ask for help.

Let me set the stage for you. Judas has already slipped into the night to join the religious leaders and temple guards, as per their agreement. The eleven disciples followed Jesus as He moved through the dark streets toward Gethsemane. They were whispering among themselves. They had never seen Him like this—nearly incoherent with grief. Finally they entered the garden and made their way to a small clearing where He bid them to sit. Turning to Peter, James, and John, He motioned for them to follow Him. He stumbled as He made His way deeper into the garden and seemed about to collapse. Finally He turned to them and, although He could hardly speak, He said, "My soul is overwhelmed with sorrow to the point of death. Stay here and keep watch with me" (Matt. 26:38).

He then withdrew from them about a stone's throw. When He was alone He fell face down and cried out to God, "My Father, if it is possible, may this cup be taken from me..." (Matt. 26:39).

Luke adds, "And being in anguish, he prayed more earnestly, and his sweat was like drops of blood falling to the ground" (Luke 22:44).

Given the circumstances, I can't help asking myself why Jesus wanted Peter, James, and John with Him. What could they do? They couldn't drink that dreadful cup for Him, nor could their prayers, no matter how desperate or faith-filled, alter Father God's eternal plan. So what was the point?

Unfortunately, that's what many of us conclude when our world is falling apart. Why bother our friends, we reason. There's nothing they can do. Can they get our job back, or restore our marriage, or heal the terminal illness that is stealing life from us? Not hardly!

I can't fault that logic but it misses the point. While a friend may not be able to put your world back together, their presence can give you the strength to do what you could never do alone and their prayers can sustain you as nothing else can. When your world is falling apart the smallest gesture—a kind word, an arm around the shoulders, or even a telephone call— take on unprecedented significance.

As I mentioned in chapter one, my sister is battling stage three Cancer. Eric, her son-in-law, started a group on Facebook called "Let's Help Sherry Beat Cancer." In a matter of a few days, more than two hundred people had joined the group and many posted encouraging messages and prayers. One evening when Sherry and her husband were feeling low they decided to check it out. As they read the posts the outpouring of love overwhelmed them. By the time they finished reading their faith had been renewed. When my sister told me about her experience I decided to read the posts for myself. Much to my disappointment I found them redundant and not all that inspiring.

What was going on? Why did Sherry and Tom find the posts so meaningful while I found them prosaic at best? When you're in a life and death struggle like they are, every encouraging word, no matter how cliché, becomes a source of strength and hope. To me the postings were just words, but to Sherry and Tom they were a lifeline!

Although I've never faced anything close to what Sherry is facing, I have had my own challenges, and in those times I have found the presence of a true friend invaluable. About five years ago, early one Friday morning, I was boarding a flight out of

Northwest Arkansas Regional Airport en route to Chicago when I was overcome with grief. Brenda's father was dying, our daughter was seriously ill with an undiagnosed disease, and my father was in poor health and not expected to live long. For months I had continued my demanding ministry schedule, never once allowing myself to grieve, but that morning it caught up with me. Although I managed to hold it together until I got off the plane, I barely made it to the men's room before breaking down.

I was scheduled to lead a Men's Conference in Cleveland that weekend and the first session was just hours away. If I didn't get a hold of myself I would be in no condition to minister. I thought about calling someone but whom could I call? And what would I tell them, that I was having an emotional breakdown? I don't think so. Besides, what could anyone do? There was no way they could fix the things that were ripping my heart out. Regardless of how bad I was hurting, I would just have to tough it out.

For the better part of an hour, I wondered the crowded terminals but found no relief. Spotting a Starbucks, I bought a Latte with an extra shot of espresso and sat down at a table by the window overlooking the tarmac. I tried to read but it was no use. My mind kept filling up with pictures of sickness and death. I saw Brenda's father wasting away with Cancer. Worse was the thought that Leah might die. I tried to imagine what would happen if she did. Who would take care of those two precious children? How would Doug manage? I tried to thrust those morbid thoughts out of my mind but it was no use. I was no match for the grief that had laid siege to my soul.

Thinking some food might help, I found a restaurant near my departure gate and ordered breakfast, but when it came I couldn't choke it down. In desperation, I decided to call John and Evelyn. They were ministerial colleagues and our friendship spanned more than twenty years. If anyone could understand what was happening to me they could.

After finding a semi-private corner in a nearly empty departure lounge, I punched their number into my cell phone. Jamming it against my ear I listened as it rang once, twice, three times. When Evelyn finally answered I tried to speak but all I could manage was a strangled whisper. Realizing something was wrong, she handed the phone to her husband and went into the office to pick up the extension.

For the next twenty minutes I poured out my pain in nearly incoherent bits and spurts. John and Evelyn didn't have any answers, not that I expected them to, but they had something better—a compassionate presence. Not once did they make light of my grief or try to comfort me with a cliché. Instead they let me talk. And after a time the raw edge of my grief began to dull. Little by little sorrow loosed its stranglehold, and when I finally ran down they prayed with me.

My circumstances didn't suddenly change. Ben still had Cancer and Leah remained desperately ill, but I was different. My heart still hurt and it would for a long time, but grief no longer paralyzed me. By allowing me to process my grief without fear of recrimination or rejection, John and Evelyn had opened the door for my healing. In the ensuing months their friendship would prove a continual source of spiritual strength and emotional support, enabling me to minister with effectiveness even as I contended with the grief of watching those I loved suffer and die.

I don't know who your "John and Evelyn" are, but whoever they are I encourage you to ask for their help—the sooner, the better. Even though they can't put your world back together, their emotional support and their prayers will prove invaluable; so don't try to go it alone. Remember, it is not weakness but wisdom that causes us to ask for help. If Jesus needed a friend when His world was falling apart, then how much more do you and I. If He couldn't go it alone then why do we think we can?

"Two are better than one,
    because they have a good return
    for their work:
If one falls down,
    His friend can help him up.
    But pity the man who falls
    and has no one to help him up!
Also, if two lie down together, they
will keep warm.
    But how can one keep warm alone?
Though one may be overpowered,
    two can defend themselves.
    A cord of three strands is not
    quickly broken."

ECCLESIASTES 4:9-12

PRAYER

Lord Jesus, even though it feels like my world is falling apart I want to thank You for all the good memories I have. I thank You for rare and tender moments – falling in love and getting married, giving birth, becoming a grandparent, growing old with the one I love. I thank You for a good marriage where love was true. I thank You for the gift of family, for three generation holidays and the running laughter of healthy grandchildren. I thank You for the comfort of friends and the strength of Scripture in the dark hour of unspeakable need. I thank You for Your faithfulness and the promise of Your presence. I thank You for turning my grief into gratefulness. With Your help I will praise You all the days of my life. In Your holy name I pray. Amen.

CHAPTER 3

RUN TO THE ROCK

"The LORD is my rock,

my fortress and my deliverer;

my God is my rock,

in whom I take refuge.

He is my shield and the horn of

my salvation,

My stronghold.

PSALMS 18:2

⸻∞⸻

"The name of the Lord is a strong tower;

the righteous run to it and are safe."

PROVERBS 18:10

RUN TO THE ROCK

I n this world you will have trouble. There's no escaping it. You may sail blissfully along for a number of years, but sooner or later something will happen to rock your world. When it does you will be shaken to the core. That's not to say your faith will fail but only that you will be stretched to the breaking point. Adversity usually comes in bunches. You get hit with one thing after another. Just when you think you are about to get back on your feet, trouble blindsides you again.

Consider what happened to a close friend of mine. His company was forced into bankruptcy and since he had personally guaranteed several of the company loans, he was forced to file personal bankruptcy as well. During this enormously stressful time his wife had two major surgeries. Just when it seemed the end was in sight, the Bankruptcy Court approved the sale of the company and the new owners dismissed him. On top of all of that, his fifty-eight year old brother-in-law dropped dead of a heart attack.

Sounds a lot like Job, doesn't it. In a single day he lost everything. Thieves stole his livestock and killed his servants. What the thieves didn't take a freak storm destroyed. And then a tornado hit the house where his children were having a dinner party, killing all of them. A short time later he was afflicted with painful boils from the top of his head to the soles of his feet. In a fit of despair, his wife urged him to curse God and die. And the final straw was when his friends suggested that he had brought all of this on himself.

If you've ever been in a situation like that you know how easy it is to become discouraged. Nothing you do seems to make any difference. You fast and pray, search your heart before God, and surrender unconditionally to Him and still nothing changes. Although you try not to, you find yourself avoiding your friends. Your presence is an embarrassment to them, or so it seems to you. Truth be known, you are an embarrassment to yourself. How could you have made such a mess of things?

You are thankful for those special spiritual friends who have stood with you, but there is a limit to what they can do. As critical as they have been to this point, you now need something more, something that only God can provide. But here's where it gets sticky. Although you would never say it out loud, your faith isn't what it once was. Too many of the things you once believed haven't worked out. You don't want to doubt God so you end up blaming yourself. The fault is not His, you conclude, but yours. You're to blame.

Stop right there! Take that thought captive. Bring it into submission to Jesus Christ. (See 2 Cor.10:3-5.) Yes, the mess you are in may be of your own making, at least partially. If so, acknowledge it. If it goes beyond poor judgment to disobedience, confess it as sin and receive His forgiveness. Then put it behind you. Remember, "…he is faithful and just and will forgive us our sins and purify us from all unrighteousness" (1 John 1:9).

Now stop berating yourself. There is nothing to be gained by continually reliving your mistakes. God has forgiven you so let them go. Remember the lessons you've learned but put your mistakes behind you and get on with your life.

Of course, getting on with your life may consist of nothing more than trudging through the mess, at least for a while. But no matter how tough it gets don't give up. Even if your faith is weak and you are tempted to question God, don't give up. When Jesus was at His lowest point and His soul was exceedingly sorrowful to the point of death He went to the Father. (See Matt. 26:38-39.) Even when God refused to grant His petition, Jesus still chose to trust Him. Make no mistake about it—it was His choice.

Trusting God is easy when everything is going well, but let your world come apart at the seams and the enemy will tempt you to blame God. When my grandson was just a little guy he was always crashing into things and hurting himself. But instead of running to us for comfort, he would run away. And if we tried to comfort him, he would strike out at us screaming, "Don't touch me. Leave me alone!"

Although we were not in any way responsible for his pain, he blamed us. I cannot help thinking how like him we are when troubles come our way. Let life deal us a crushing blow and we are quick to blame God. We are tempted to question His goodness and to scold Him for the "injustices" we are suffering.

But you don't have to respond that way. You have a choice. You can respond like my grandson responded to us when he was hurt, or you can respond like Jesus did in Gethsemane. You can push God away or you can cling to Him, putting your trust in Him and Him alone. Of course you continue to pray for a miracle but your hope is in God and God alone.

You may be tempted to think that God doesn't care, especially given the fact that your world continues to come apart no matter how hard you pray. Don't go there. Don't question God. It's a dead end. Instead, run to the Father and throw yourself into His arms. Let Him hold you and comfort you. Surrender your "why" questions and simply rest in Him.

Meditate on what it means for God to be your Father. Think about your feelings for your children. Surely nothing pains you more than seeing one of them suffer nor does anything bless you more than their happiness. Whatever touches them touches you. If you, a mere mortal, have these kinds of feelings for your children then just imagine how much more Father God cares for you. Psalms 103:13 says, "As a father has compassion on his children, so the LORD has compassion on those who fear him."

I am especially sensitive to this truth at the moment because my sister is battling stage three Cancer. No matter what I am doing, Sherry's situation is never far from my mind. When I lie in bed at night awaiting sleep, my mind is searching for solutions. My first thought upon waking in the morning is a prayer for her. When I pray, her needs take precedence over almost everything else. I am her brother, and I am touched by the feelings of her infirmities. What hurts her hurts me. Her pain is my pain. Yet as much as I care about Sherry, I know that if it were my daughter battling Cancer my concern would be even greater. Nothing other than God's love can compare to what a loving parent feels for his/her children.

Now let's take that one step further. Is not my concern for Sherry but a dim reflection of Father God's concern for her and for us? "If you, then, though you are evil, know how to give good gifts to your children, how much more will your Father in heaven give good gifts to those who ask Him!" (Matt. 7:11).

Here's where I struggle. If God is touched by the things that touch me, then why doesn't He do something about it? Why hasn't He healed my sister? Why make her go through the horrors of chemotherapy? She will have to be in the hospital seven days at a time and, according to the oncologists, she can expect to experience bloating, vomiting, diarrhea, and severe flu like symptoms, unless of course she has a severe reaction to the drugs. Then things could get really bad. After all of that the doctors give her no more than a fifty percent chance of beating the Cancer. Surely Father God takes no pleasure in my sister's suffering, so why doesn't He do something?

Herein lies the tension in which we live, especially when our world is crashing down around us. On the one hand we have the clear teaching of Scripture portraying God as an all-powerful heavenly Father who is eager to intervene on our behalf. On the other hand, we are confronted with the reality of painful situations that seem immune to our most desperate prayers. If God genuinely cares, if He is truly touched by the feelings of our infirmities, why doesn't He intervene? Why doesn't He do something?

I've heard all the explanations: God makes decisions based on the big picture, the eternal perspective, and not on our limited understanding. God is more concerned about our character and eternal well being than our physical comfort. God loves us enough to let us struggle for a season, if need be, in order to fulfill His purpose in our lives. God allows some things to happen to us in order to do something in us so He can do something through us.

That makes sense to me intellectually, but on an emotional level I struggle with it, especially when I think of my sister and what she's facing. I don't want to take the long view, the eternal perspective. I just want God to heal her.

Don't misunderstand me. When I say God allows things to happen to us so He can do something through us, I am not suggesting that He caused Sherry's illness or that He willed it. He may have allowed it, I don't know, but I am certain He will redeem it. He will touch it with His grace and bring eternal good out of what appears at the moment to be nothing more than a senseless tragedy. That's what I choose to believe but it isn't easy. Still it is the only way.

I believe that God will redeem my sister's situation and yours because He has a long history of turning the tables on the enemy. More often than not, He takes the very things the enemy intends to use to destroy us and turns them into instruments of grace. He uses them to further His eternal purposes in our lives and in our world. Therefore, in the face of illness and adversity, we affirm "…that in all things God works for the good of those who love him, who have been called according to his purpose" (Rom. 8:28). I wish I could say that I know this means Sherry will be healed, but I can't. Still, I take comfort knowing God is in control.

That doesn't mean I understand why this is happening, but I am convinced that Father God loves my sister more than I ever could. I believe with all my heart that He is too loving to ever allow her to suffer needless pain and too wise to ever make a mistake. If we could see what He sees, that is, if we had all the "facts," I am convinced it would make sense to us. So why doesn't He explain it to us?

As I grapple with these thoughts, I'm reminded of a young couple who were expecting their first child. They wanted everything to be perfect and prayed accordingly. They prayed that their baby would have perfect health, a gentle disposition, and a spiritual aptitude. According to their theology, this should have assured them of a perfect child. Imagine their bewilderment when their newborn daughter cried incessantly. In addition to the obvious concern they had for her well being, they were also tormented with self-doubt and questions regarding their faith.

In desperation they came to see me. "Pastor," they demanded, "why did God not answer our prayers? We prayed in faith. We did everything we were taught to do, so why didn't it work?"

A fair enough question and one for which I had no ready answer. Besides they were not ready to receive any explanation I might have offered, so I just shrugged my shoulders. As they prepared to leave my office, I assured them of God's love and faithfulness but I could tell they were far from satisfied.

A few weeks later the doctor discovered that their baby had a hernia, which explained the baby's incessant crying, but only complicated their crisis of faith. Surgery was scheduled and when the appointed day arrived I went to the hospital to be with them. Long before I located the parents I could hear the baby wailing. Her anguished cries echoed forlornly down the long hospital corridors. Turning a final corner, I saw the young mother nervously pacing the hallway trying to comfort her baby daughter, while her husband looked on helplessly.

Approaching her I asked, "What seems to be the problem?"

"She's hungry," the distraught mother replied. "The doctor told us not to feed her after ten o'clock last night."

"Surely you're not going to let that stop you?" I asked with a straight face.

"What do you mean?" she asked, puzzled.

"Your baby is obviously hungry and not to feed her is terribly cruel."

She looked at me like I had lost my mind. Finally she said, "Surely you know how dangerous it is to have surgery on a full stomach, especially for a baby."

Without giving her a chance to finish I interrupted. "Well, at least explain that to her. She must think you're a sadist. You carry her in your arms next to your breast, but you won't feed her. As young as she is she knows you could feed her if you wanted to, if you really cared."

"Don't be silly," she said with forced calmness, "you can't explain something like that to a three-month-old baby."

She started to turn away and then understanding brightened her features. Turning back to me she said, "You're not really talking about my baby and me are you?"

Gently I replied, "I know what you are doing is an act of love. I know you have your baby's best interest at heart and so do you. But she doesn't understand that, and you're right, there's no way you can explain it to her."

She was listening intently now, so I continued, "That's the way it is with God. He is divine while we are merely human. He is infinite while we are finite. His thoughts are not our thoughts, nor are His ways our ways. (See Isa. 55:8-9). It would be easier for your three-month-old daughter to grasp the logic of your love in not feeding her when she is hungry, than it would be for us to grasp the infinite wisdom of God. There are times when we simply have to trust God's heart even if we can't understand His ways."

Like that young couple, you may be facing a crisis right now, and like them you may be asking why. You may even be tempted to rail at God about the apparent injustice of life, the unfairness of it all. Don't. That is just an exercise in futility. Instead, encourage yourself in the Lord. (See 1 Sam. 30:6.) Strengthen your faith by affirming your confidence in God's goodness, in His sufficiency, and in His willingness to do what is best for you. Accept the fact that in this life we only "...see through a glass darkly...[we only] know in part..." (1 Cor. 13:12 KJV).

We began this chapter by looking at the trouble Job suffered and I would like to close it by considering what he did when his world was falling apart. From a human perspective the tragedies that befell him made absolutely no sense. According to the biblical record he "...was blameless and upright; he feared God and shunned evil" (Job 1:1). To our way of thinking that should have protected him from trouble, but it didn't. His friends suggested that he had brought the trouble on himself and his wife urged him to curse God and die, but Job refused to reject God. Although his suffering made no sense to him, and he could not understand why his world was suddenly falling apart, he still trusted God. Through clinched teeth he declared his faith, "Though he slay me, yet will I trust in him" (Job 13:15 KJV).

Even when it looked like he would never escape his poverty or his sickness, even when it appeared he would die in his shame, he refused to turn his back on God. By faith he looked beyond his circumstances, even beyond the grave, and declared, "I know that my Redeemer lives, and that in the end he will stand upon the earth. And after my skin has been destroyed, yet in my flesh I will see God; I myself will see him with my own eyes—I, and not another" (Job 19:25-27).

There were moments when Job railed at God and questioned His goodness, but in the end he realized the wisdom of God was beyond his understanding and he submitted to it. "Surely I spoke of things I did not understand, things too wonderful for me to know.

Therefore I despise myself and repent in dust and ashes" (Job 42:3,6). And because Job remained faithful no matter what, God restored his good fortune "...and gave him twice as much as he had before" (Job 42:10).

Although we are separated from him by centuries, even millenniums, I can almost hear him say, "Trust God in your darkest hour. Trust Him when it makes no sense, when all the evidence says He has let you down. Trust Him even when the heavens turn to brass and your most desperate prayers go unanswered. Trust Him no matter what. Trust God unconditionally and He will grant you a supernatural peace that is not dependent on either circumstances or understanding. "And the peace of God, which transcends all understanding, will guard your hearts and your minds in Christ Jesus" (Phil. 4:7).

PRAYER

Lord Jesus, it's easy to dance when life is filled with music and laughter but I want to learn to dance when the lights go out and the laughter is gone. If I'm going to dance in the darkness I will have to cling more tightly to You, follow Your lead more closely, especially when I can't hear the music. But if I can do this I will discover a strength that those who only dance in the light will never know. Dance with me in the darkness, Lord Jesus. In Your holy name I pray. Amen.

CHAPTER 4

DRINK THE CUP

"Three times I pleaded with the Lord to take it away from me. But he said to me, 'My grace is sufficient for you, for my power is made perfect in weakness.' Therefore I will boast all the more gladly about my weaknesses, so that Christ's power may rest on me. That is why, for Christ's sake, I delight in weaknesses, in insults, in hardships, in persecutions, in difficulties. For when I am weak, then I am strong."

2 CORINTHIANS 12:8-10

DRINK THE CUP

In Gethsemane Jesus wrestled with the same kind of emotions we struggle with when our world comes crashing down, only on a scale that dwarfs anything we have ever faced. Have you been betrayed? So was He. Have your friends let you down? He knows what that's like. Have you been misunderstood? Ditto for Him. Have you been falsely accused? He was too. Is your future filled with peril? So was His. Are you facing things you can't control? He was too. Are you facing physical suffering and imminent death? He's been there. I could continue but I think you get the point. You're not up against anything Jesus hasn't already been through.

I can almost hear you saying, "Yes, but He is different. He may have been a man but He was also God incarnate."

You are absolutely right. Jesus was both the Son of God and the Son of man but that doesn't mean He didn't suffer as all men suffer. When He lived among us He was not God in a human disguise, rather He was fully human. "In all things He had to be made like His brethren" (Heb. 2:17 NKJV).

The apostle Paul explained it this way: "His state was divine, yet he did not cling to his equality with God **but emptied himself** to assume the condition of a slave, and became as men are; and being as all men are, he was humbler yet, even to accepting death, death on a cross" (Phil. 2:6-8 *Jerusalem Bible*, emphasis mine).

Although Jesus was in every way one with God, He "emptied" Himself and became one of us. He did not empty Himself of His divine nature or essence rather, He "stripped himself of every privilege" (Phil. 2:7 Phillips). That is, He voluntarily relinquished every advantage of His divine nature in order to become a full-fledged human being. He was still divine but He freely chose to live as a man in order to fulfill the righteous requirements of the Father's holy law. And because He lived, suffered, and was tempted as a man He is able to help us in the hour of our temptation. (See Heb. 2:17,18.)

Another thing that makes it hard for us to comprehend the reality of the battle that Jesus waged in Gethsemane is the fact that we see it in light of the resurrection. We know the end of the story and in a very real sense that robs it of some of its gut wrenching impact. We would do well to remember that when Jesus was sweating blood in Gethsemane the resurrection was only a faith reality for Him, not a historical fact. It was something He believed but had not yet experienced. Ultimately it gave Him the strength and courage to surrender to the Father's will, but it did not neutralize the spiritual and emotional conflict He experienced. In fact, the conflict between His will and the Father's will generated so much internal dissonance that He sweat great drops of blood (see Luke 22:44) and feared for His very life. (See Matt. 26:38.) Who knows what might have happened if an angel hadn't come and strengthened Him. (See Luke 22:43.)

Gethsemane was not only a place of suffering that final night but also a place of mystery. We see a side of Jesus we have never seen before; a side we never knew existed. Heretofore He has always been quick to do the Father's will, but on this night everything within Him is repulsed by the course the Father has set before Him. Instead of praying for strength and courage He pleads with God to take the cup from Him. Desperately, He searches for an alternative, for another way, a less extreme way, to fulfill the Father's purpose.

It was not the Father's purpose that troubled Jesus but the process necessary to accomplish it. He was fully committed to the Father's purpose, which was the salvation of Adam's lost race, but He begged Father God to reconsider the process. Surely there was another way, a less extreme way. "My Father," He prayed, "if it is possible, may this cup be taken from me. Yet not as I will, but as you will" (Matt. 26:39).

Jesus knew what lay before Him—betrayal and arrest, desertion and denial, false accusations and an unjust conviction on a charge of blasphemy. His own countrymen will scream for His blood. Pilate will order Him scourged, and He will be beaten within an inch of His life. Finally, the Romans will nail Him to a cross, and there He will die.

All of this was painful beyond imagination; yet it was not more than His soul could bear. It was not what He pleaded for the Father to take from Him. All of this He could endure because the Father would be with Him. God would strengthen Him. With the Father's help He could bear the injustice and brutality of men. What He could not imagine, what His soul cringed at, was the prospect of being separated from the Father and suffering the penalty for sin at His hand.

Once more the Father pressed the cup upon Him, and try as He might, Jesus could not bring Himself to drink it. In its dark dregs was the poison that was destroying those who were created in His image. There was rebellion, and lust, and profane passions. It was filled to the brim with all manner of evil—treachery and deceit, pride and power, adultery and murder. Sickness and disease were there, as was death. Everything that He hated was in that cup, everything that He had come to destroy.

The Father's purpose was clear, but Jesus could not bring Himself to accept His plan, at least not yet. Surely there must be another way. "Father," He prayed, while His inner turmoil caused His sweat to become like blood, "if it is not possible for this cup to be taken away unless I drink it, may your will be done" (Matt. 26:42).

Having said that, He fled the place of prayer to seek the support of His friends. Once more He found them sleeping, and though His heart was grieved He did not wake them. Their companionship might provide a temporary solace, but in the end the cup was His and His alone. No one could drink it for Him.

For the third time He went to the Father, His anguish nearly more than He could bear, and He prayed even more earnestly with tears and loud cries. (See Heb. 5:7.) Having exhausted every other recourse, He finally acknowledged that there was no other way. In order to destroy the thing He hates above all else He will have to drink the cup of iniquity. Although He has been tempted in all ways without succumbing to sin, (see Heb. 4:15) He must now voluntarily become sin (see 2 Cor. 5:21) in order to accomplish the Father's purpose. With trembling hands He took the cup from the Father and placed it to His lips. "May your will be done," He prayed, and drank deeply from its deadly dregs.

Instantly a supernatural peace filled His being. No longer was He at war with himself or the Father. Once more He was centered. His only reason for living was to accomplish the Father's purpose. Like a flint, He set His face toward Golgotha.

The next twelve hours were horrible beyond imagination. Jesus suffered in every way it is possible for a human being to suffer—physically, mentally, and emotionally. From a human perspective His world continued to fall apart, but the supernatural peace He had received when He submitted to the Father's will never wavered.

Someone has suggested that when your world is falling apart you have three choices: you can curse life for doing this to you and look for some way to express your grief and rage; you can grit your teeth and endure it; or you can accept it. To my way of thinking there is really only one option—acceptance. Not resignation, which gives up and says, "Whatever will be will be." But acceptance, which submits to the Father's will even when there is not so much as a hint of deliverance in sight. Acceptance enables you to pray for a miracle while leaving the nature of the miracle to the wisdom of God. Your miracle may come as supernatural deliverance, or it may come as special grace to live with meaning even as you come to grips with the tragedy that is unfolding.

Another way to view acceptance is to think of it as surrender. When Jesus prayed, "...not as I will, but as you will" (Matt. 26:39), He was accepting the Father's plan even as He surrendered His hopes and dreams of persuading God to find a different, easier way to redeem Adam's lost race.

Given your current crisis what do you need to surrender? If you have suffered a devastating loss you are probably dealing with a host of painfully destructive emotions. Maybe you have been taught that a "real" Christian shouldn't feel the kind of things you're feeling and if they do they shouldn't acknowledge those feelings. If so, you're probably condemning yourself for feeling the way you do.

Given this scenario many people try to repress their feelings, but that can be spiritually and emotionally exhausting. It's like trying to hold a beach ball under water. You can do it but it takes tremendous concentration, and if you relax for a second the beach ball pops out of the water.

So what is the solution? You can vent your feelings, just let it all "hang out" as we used to say, but that can be pretty destructive. It may relieve the pressure for the moment but it doesn't resolve anything. The emotional pressure soon builds back up and you will find yourself venting again. If you're not careful you will get stuck in that self-destructive cycle and your volatile emotions will turn you into the kind of person others avoid.

Since neither repressing your destructive emotions nor expressing them really works, what can you do? You can accept them for what they are and then surrender them to God. In prayer tell Him how angry you are that this is happening to you and to those you love. Tell Him how disappointed you are that He hasn't intervened on your behalf. Tell Him how unfair you think it is. Tell Him that you can't understand why He would heal someone else when He hasn't healed you. Tell Him whatever you are thinking or feeling. Get it all out. Don't hold anything back.

Now tell Him that you don't want to feel that way but you can't seem to help yourself. Give Him permission to change your feelings. Ask Him to "tune" your emotions until they are "pitched" to His perfect will. Ask Him to help you base your emotions on who He is rather than on your circumstances. Ask Him to do for you what you cannot do for yourself. As you linger quietly in His presence consciously choose to release your negative emotions. Let them go. Surrender them to Him. Allow His peace to fill those empty places where fear and anger once lived.

Following the premature death of his young wife one grieving husband prayed, "God, I love you, but I'm really angry right now. I don't want to feel this way, but I can't seem to help myself. The doctors did everything they could, but in the end they were powerless. I did everything I could and still my beloved died. Had I done any less I would have never been able to forgive myself. You are the only one who did nothing, or so it seems to me. You have the power of life and death and yet You did not intervene. You could have prevented the accident but You didn't. Failing there, You could have healed her but You didn't. All of us, who have such limited power, did everything we could but it feels like You, who have all power, did nothing at all. I'm trying to understand why You didn't do anything, but right now I can't."

Had this grieving husband been unable or unwilling to surrender his toxic emotions to Father God they would have poisoned his faith and turned him into a prematurely old and bitter man. As it was, once he was able to release his hurt and anger, once he was able to surrender his bitter feelings to the Lord, God was able to begin the healing process.

Sometime later he was able to pray: "Father God, hurt and anger were making me bitter, killing the relationship we once shared. I wanted to punish You, yet even in my anger I knew You were my only hope. With one hand I pushed You away while with the other hand I clung to You with all my might. With a trembling faith I lifted my hurt to You, trusting that You would take it from me. And You did. You replaced my anger with acceptance, my hurt with hope. I know I will never understand why things happened the way they did, but in spite of that I choose to trust You. You are my Lord and my God and I will serve You. Amen."

Of course negative emotions may not be the only thing you need to surrender. You may also need to give God your predetermined expectations—that is, your hopes and dreams. I want to be very careful here because the Scriptures teach that we have not because we ask not (see James 4:2), so there is a place for specific prayers. Yet the Scriptures also say that we ask and do not receive because we ask for the wrong things or with the wrong motive. (See James 4:3.) I would like to suggest that even as you pray with faith for specific answers, you also humbly submit to the will of the Father, acknowledging that you don't truly know how you should pray. (See Rom. 8:26, 27.)

This is where Jesus found Himself that final night in Gethsemane. Matthew tells us, "he fell with his face to the ground and prayed, 'My Father, if it is possible, may this cup be taken from me…'" (Matt. 26:39). That was a very specific prayer but God did not grant it. In fact, the harder Jesus prayed the more distressed He became. "And being in anguish, he prayed more earnestly, and his sweat was like drops of blood falling to the ground" (Luke 22:44). As long as Jesus prayed for the Father to remove the cup His inner turmoil intensified. He found peace only when He surrendered His expectations, only when He prayed, "My Father, if it is not possible for this cup to be taken away unless I drink it, may your will be done" (Matt. 26:42).

Throughout your crisis you have undoubtedly been praying very specific prayers. Like Jesus in Gethsemane, you know exactly what you want God to do. You have asked Him to restore your finances. You have asked Him to sell your home before you lose it to foreclosure. You have asked Him to give you a good paying job. Or maybe you have been praying for your marriage. Maybe you have been asking Him to heal the deep wounds in your relationship, to turn your spouse's heart back to you. Or maybe you have been praying for a miracle of healing. You know exactly how things need to work out and you have made it a point to pray accordingly. Unfortunately, the heavens seem to have turned to brass and the harder you pray the more agitated you become.

Do what Jesus did. Surrender your expectations. Give Father God all of your hopes and dreams for the future. You can trust Him; you really can. He loves you absolutely and He has your best interest at heart. And He is "…able to do immeasurably more than all we ask or imagine…" (Eph. 3:20). When I was just a young man an older preacher gave me some counsel I never forgot. He said, "If you leave the choice up to God He will always give you His best."

Some years ago a couple came to me for prayer at the end of service. They were childless and in their late 30s or early 40s. When they approached me the woman was weeping. "I don't want you to pray for me," she sobbed, "but you must!" Then she proceeded to tell me that neither prayer nor medicine had been helpful. After nearly twenty years of trying they had lost all hope of ever having children of their own.

Having finally surrendered their desires to God, they were able to make a tentative peace with their situation. If they couldn't have children of their own they would simply love the children God had placed in their life—their nieces and nephews, as well as the boys and girls in her Sunday school class. She told me she could live without children but what she couldn't bear was to get her hopes up only to be disappointed yet again. That's why she didn't want me to pray for her, then she quickly added, "But I feel you must pray for me!"

Taking both of her hands in mine, I prayed earnestly but my expectations weren't very high. Suddenly the Holy Spirit came upon me and I heard myself saying, "About this time next year the Lord will give you a son."

Once I had uttered those words I was dumbfounded. What was I thinking? How dare I speak so presumptuously? How dare I give them false hopes?

But it turns out that I hadn't given them false hopes. Twelve months later she gave birth to a healthy baby boy! How do I explain that? I can't.

They had been prayed for scores of times across the years without ever conceiving a child. What was different this time? She didn't appear to have much faith—a desperate hope maybe, but not much faith. My faith certainly wasn't anything to write home about, but God still intervened and gave them a son. Maybe when they stopped demanding a child of their own and simply accepted their situation God intervened. How did the old preacher put it? "When you leave the choice up to Him God always gives you His best!"

I know God is able, and I have witnessed enough supernatural interventions to never lose hope no matter how desperate the situation. Yet, I've preached enough funerals that I dare not be presumptuous. Christ has defeated death but He has not yet destroyed it (see 1 Cor. 15:26), and until He does we will have to contend with both sickness and death. Here's what I've determined to do anytime my world seems to be falling apart: I'm going to surrender my situation to Father God praying, "Not my will but yours be done." Then I'm going to pray for a miracle, but I'm going to put my hope in God and God alone. If you put your hope in a miracle you may be disappointed, but if you put your hope in God, He will never let you down.

The pain we experience in the midst of personal tragedy is often compounded by our stubborn refusal to make peace with our situation. Instead of trusting God and surrendering to His purposes, we often demand a miracle. As a result we end up "sweating blood." The inner turmoil that is tearing us apart is not caused by the external circumstances in which we find ourselves as much as it is caused by the battle our will is waging against the Father's will. And we can't get beyond this place until we are willing to drink the cup.

Let me encourage you to pray the prayer Jesus prayed in Gethsemane right now. "My Father, if it is not possible for this cup to be taken away unless I drink it, may your will be done" (Matt. 26:42).

Did you pray that prayer? How do you feel now? Are you at peace?

Maybe you still can't fully surrender to the Father's will. Don't be discouraged. Jesus couldn't do it the first time He prayed either. In fact He had to pray three times before He could fully surrender to the Father's will.

Take a moment and see if you can identify what's holding you back. Is it fear or stubbornness? Is it pride? Whatever it is, I want you to consciously choose to surrender it to the Father. Now let's pray again: "My

Father, if it is not possible for this cup to be taken away unless I drink it, may your will be done."

How do you feel now? Are you still struggling?

Okay let's try it one more time. Remember, you are not giving up. You are not quitting. You are simply surrendering to Father God. You are acknowledging that He is wiser than you are, that He knows best. "My Father, if it is not possible for this cup to be taken away unless I drink it, may your will be done."

Now, by faith, I want you to see yourself kneeling before the Father in humble submission. Take the cup from His hand and drink it. Let the Father's peace and His presence fill your soul. Now your will and the Father's will are one and you can face the future, whatever it holds, without fear. Hear the Father say:

> "You are my servant;
>> I have chosen you and have not
>> rejected you.

So do not fear, for I am with you;
>   do not be dismayed, for I am
>   your God.
>   I will strengthen you and help you;
>   I will uphold you with my right-
>   eous right hand.
All who rage against you
>   will surely be ashamed
>   and disgraced;
>   those who oppose you
>   will be as nothing and perish.
Though you search for you enemies,
>   you will not find them.
>   Those who wage war against you
>   will be as nothing at all.
For I am the LORD, your God,
>   who takes hold of your right hand
>   and says to you, Do not fear;
>   I will help you."

ISAIAH 41:9-13

PRAYER

Lord Jesus, I don't want to feel this way, I don't want to question Your love or Your wisdom, but I can't seem to help myself. Pain and disappointment have turned me into a conflicted person. With one hand I shove you away and with the other I cling to You for dear life. Help me to trust You even if I cannot understand Your ways for You are my only hope, my only help. In Your holy name I pray. Amen.

CHAPTER 5

TURNING TRAGEDY INTO TRIUMPH

"We were under great pressure, far beyond our ability to endure, so that we despaired even of life. Indeed, in our hearts we felt the sentence of death. But this happened that we might not rely on ourselves but on God, who raises the dead. He had delivered us from such a deadly peril, and he will deliver us. On him we have set our hope that he will continue to deliver us...."

2 CORINTHIANS 1:8-10

TURNING TRAGEDY INTO TRIUMPH

———⚬⚬⚬———

Wh.en Jesus left the place of prayer that final time and returned to His sleeping disciples, His internal storm was over. Having surrendered to the Father's will He was at peace in the core of His being. Unfortunately the external storm was building, and through the shadowy darkness He could see the flickering torches of the temple guards as they approached, with Judas in the forefront. How like our own lives this is. Even when we have fully surrendered to the Father, the external storms continue to rage, sometimes for a long time. He has given us a deep-seated peace, an assurance that He has everything under control, but our circumstances still look just as grim and foreboding.

A common tendency at this point is to give your peace away. It doesn't seem right or natural to be so unconcerned. Logic tells you that given your situation you should be more anxious, more concerned about the future. You are tempted to wonder if you are in denial or if you are just too exhausted to care anymore. If you are not careful you will begin focusing on your circumstances rather than His sufficiency, and when you do anxiety will begin to seep back into your soul, even fear.

During my sister's ongoing battle against Cancer she has possessed a remarkable peace and an unshakable faith. That is not to say she hasn't had moments when thoughts of dying and leaving her family haven't filled her mind and tempted her to fear, but to this point she has been able to bring those tormenting thoughts into subjection to Christ. (See 2 Cor. 10:3-5.) As long as she allows the Holy Spirit to direct her thoughts her faith remains strong, but if she lets down her guard for even a moment, fear comes rushing in.

You've probably experienced the same thing in your own life. Focus on the Lord and your faith remains strong no matter how difficult your circumstances. Focus on your situation and fear returns with a vengeance.

So what does this teach us?

True peace, that inner calm that transcends all understanding, has little or nothing to do with our circumstances. It comes from the Prince of Peace. Draw near to Him, saturate your heart and mind with His presence, and you will experience a profound peace even when your world is falling apart. Well did the prophet say, "Thou wilt keep him in perfect peace, whose mind is stayed on thee, because he trusteth in thee" (Isa. 26:3 KJV).

Conversely, the source of your anxiety is not rooted in the troubles that have beset you as much as in your response to them. Jesus did not sweat blood in Gethsemane because of the cup, but because He refused to yield to the Father's will. Once He fully surrendered to the Father He was at peace. His circumstances had not changed. The future was still dark and foreboding, He still had to drink the cup, but He was at peace.

Accept what you cannot change. Surrender it to God. Place your destiny in His hands. Trust your future to Him and He will take care of you. That's what Jesus did and God turned the tragedy of the crucifixion into the glory of the resurrection!

I'm convinced that most people can overcome any life shattering adversity if they can be assured of three things. First, they must know that God cares, that He suffers with them. Then they must be convinced that God is near, that He won't forsake them, He won't leave them to wander alone through the darkness of their broken world. Finally, they have to know that God will redeem their situation; that He will make it contribute in some way to His divine purpose. As rational creatures, the thought that a tragic accident or some other life-altering event might be pointless is simply unbearable. But if we are convinced that God will ultimately bring good out of what looks like to the world like a senseless tragedy, we can somehow bear it.

Do you remember the time Jesus and His disciples got caught at sea in a terrible storm? Mark records it in chapter 4: "A furious squall came up, and the waves broke over the boat, so that it was nearly swamped. Jesus was in the stern, sleeping on a cushion. The disciples woke him and said to him, 'Teacher, don't you care if we drown?'" (vv. 37,38).

"Don't you care?"

That's the question that haunts us when our secure world is suddenly shattered. We want to know if God cares.

I'm reminded of a young couple who spent two years on the mission field. While there they had a second child who was stillborn. It was a devastating blow. They were thousands of miles from family and friends, laying their lives on the line for the sake of the kingdom, doing exactly what God had called them to do, so why did their baby die? How many times, I wonder, did they cry, "Lord, don't You care?"

A grieving mother comes to mind. Much of her life has been fraught with tragedy. She married a soldier who brought her to the United States following his tour of duty. Shortly after the birth of their first child, he left her for another woman. Alone in a strange country, with a baby to care for, she must have wondered, "Lord, don't You care?"

Her son, she soon discovered, was severely epileptic, requiring constant medication and care, plus special schooling. "Lord, don't You care?"

Finally, at the age of sixteen, the young man was enrolled in public school and it seemed that, at last, he was entering the mainstream of life. Then in a freak accident, he drowned. Out of the darkness of her grief that mother cried, "Lord, don't You care?" I know because I was her counselor.

These are extreme cases, but they are not nearly as isolated as you might think. After more than forty years in the ministry I've come to realize just how many people live with unspeakable sorrow. How many people suffer in silence and hide their hurt behind a public smile. Over and over they plead with me for an answer. "Does God care?" they ask, or, "Why doesn't God do something?"

It's not really answers they seek, but assurance. Intuitively, they know that the "why" questions are beyond us. The good news is that if we will let Him, God will give us something better than answers. He will give us trust, unconditional trust!

The real question isn't so much "Why?" but "Does God know, does He care?" And in response, all I can do is point to the Cross. There He is—God's Son—bleeding and dying because He cares! The next time you are in the midst of a crisis and tempted to cry, "Lord, don't You care?" look to the Cross. It says it all. It's all the answer we need!

Once we know God cares, then we need to be assured that He is with us. I truly believe that we can overcome any adversity, endure any hardship, if only we can know that we are not alone. The sense of God's nearness is what has kept my sister going in the face of overwhelming odds. When she is tempted to despair, to give up the fight, she strengthens herself by meditating on the Lord's nearness. I've prayed

TURNING TRAGEDY INTO TRIUMPH

with her nearly every day. We pray for a miracle of healing. We pray for strength to get through all the treatments. We pray for God to redeem this tragedy, to bring good out of this terrible ordeal. All of this is meaningful to her but what quiets her spirit and strengthens her heart is when I pray for God to be nearer to her than the breath she breaths, closer than life itself. As long as she can sense His near presence she can face her uncertain future with courage.

Like so many others who have endured unspeakable ordeals, Sherry can't bear the thought that her suffering might be pointless. If she has to endure the ravages of chemotherapy and surgery, while looking the possibility of a premature death in the eye, she wants to be assured that her suffering won't be wasted. She clings tightly to Romans 8:28: "And we know that in all things God works for the good of those who love him, who have been called according to his purpose." Unfortunately, the good God is working through our suffering is often nearly impossible to see in this life. Still, that doesn't mean that God is not at work.

I'm thinking of a pastor whose only son committed suicide. His grief nearly killed him, and during the weeks and months of darkness that followed his son's death only one thing brought him comfort— the promise of Romans 8:28. He couldn't imagine how God could bring anything good out of his son's suicide, still he clung to that verse like a drowning man clings to a life preserver.

One Lord's day he entered the pulpit and, visibly struggling, he read Romans 8:28. Under obvious duress he said, "Since my son's suicide, sleep has been mostly impossible for me and many nights I have found myself wandering the docks along the harbor, trying to understand how this could have happened. Intellectually I realize that I will probably never understand why my son took his life, but my heart cries out for an explanation. Even if I could understand why he did it, it wouldn't change a thing...."

Holding up his Bible he continued, "I cannot make my son's suicide fit into Romans 8:28. It's impossible for me to see how anything good can come out of it. But even in my grief-numbed state I realize that I only see in part and I only know in part. The scope of this verse is beyond me and somehow it supports me, it enables me to go on living even though life doesn't seem to make any sense. Even though I can't explain how, I believe when all of life is over, when God has fully worked out His will, even my son's suicide will be woven into the final tapestry of His eternal design.

"It's like the mystery, the miracle, of the shipyard. Almost every part of our great ocean-going vessels is made of steel and if you take any single part, be it a steel plate out of the hull or the huge steel rudder, and throw it into the ocean it will sink. Steel doesn't float! But when the shipbuilders are finished, when the last steel plate has been riveted into place, then that massive steel ship will float. Steel doesn't float but when the ship builders are finished it does!

"Taken by itself my son's suicide is senseless. Throw it into the ocean of Romans 8:28 and it sinks. But I believe that when the eternal shipbuilder is finally finished, when God has worked out His perfect design, even this senseless tragedy will "float." It will somehow work to our eternal good."

Maybe that's where you're at right at this moment. Your life is a mess and you can't imagine how things will ever get turned around. Nor can you imagine how any good could ever come out of the tragedies that have befallen you. Truth be told, you are ready to give up. Don't! Things may get worse before they get better, but hang in there. God will turn it around.

When Jesus walked out of Gethsemane He knew things were going to go from bad to worse, but He looked beyond the immediate tragedy to the ultimate triumph. All His disciples could see was the tragedy unfolding—a kangaroo court, a bloodthirsty mob, and a cruel death. Jesus saw all of that but He could see beyond it. And it was what He could see—"the joy set before him"—that gave Him the strength to endure the Cross. By faith He could see hundreds of millions, even billions, of blood bought people "… from every tribe and language and people and nation" (Rev. 5:9). He could see the power of sin broken, death and hell vanquished. (See Rev. 1:18.)

When you look around what do you see? A broken world filled with heartache and loss? Do you see broken dreams, a failed business, family problems and an impending divorce? That's all there plus a whole lot more. No one can deny that, but you're only seeing with one eye. If you open both eyes you will not only see what is—the tragedies of life—but what can be. If you look with the eye of faith you will see joy where you were sure there was no joy to be found and possibilities where you were sure none existed.

You might even see a miracle in the making, for with God nothing is impossible. (See Luke 1:37.)

The most profound joys I have ever witnessed, or experienced, have come in the midst of great suffering or profound loss. Consider the experience related by a remarkable woman who refuses to let life defeat her. In a two-year period she lost her mother in a fatal accident, suffered a painful and unwanted divorce, saw the last of her four children graduate and leave home. On top of all of that she was diagnosed with breast Cancer. Radical surgery followed and then chemotherapy. Since her husband had divorced her, and her children had moved away, there was no one to take care of her, so she took care of herself.

She could have succumbed to self-pity and given up, but she didn't. Instead she decided to chase her dream. Although she was weak and sick from the chemo, she enrolled at a local college, determined to get her degree if it was the last thing she ever did. As she told a friend, "I had to make a choice, to beat it or let it beat me. I decided to beat it. After all it's only Cancer!"

The road hasn't been easy. She had to take all of her classes on line between trips to the hospital for treatment. Assignments had to be completed while contending with the side effects of all the medications she was taking. Had she chosen to quit no one would have blamed her, but she wouldn't give up and now she has a college degree. More importantly, she has refused to let her circumstances determine the quality of her life. No matter how dark it gets she just keeps dancing!

Now she's facing another challenge. The doctors have discovered another spot—near the base of her skull this time, but like she says, "It's just Cancer, and between me and God we can accomplish anything." Like I said, she just keeps dancing!

The thing that makes her situation so remarkable is not the tragedy she has suffered, but the way she has chosen to respond. Instead of succumbing to self-pity or anger, she is seizing every minute and living each one to the very fullest. As a consequence she is joyously alive, albeit in the face of great adversity.

Does she grieve? Of course she does. Is she afraid? Sometimes. Especially when she thinks of her three grandchildren growing up without her, but she refuses to live in fear. If she had been given a choice, she wouldn't have chosen divorce or Cancer, but in the midst of it she has found strength she never knew she had, and an appreciation for life unlike anything she has ever known.

Life on our fallen planet is seldom easy and it is often filled with circumstances that try the strongest faith. Yet, more often than not, it is these dark times that produce the most profound and enriching experiences. For instance, a pastoral colleague has been receiving radiation therapy for stage two Cancer at MD Anderson Cancer Clinic in Houston, Texas. Although he is several hundred miles from home and away from his children he remains faith filled. In every email he tells us of the many patients and their families that he's been able to minister to. Under the most adverse circumstances he radiates joy and a Christ-like compassion that is an inspiration to all who know him.

Another friend, also a pastor, is facing nearly over-whelming challenges. His college age daughter has been diagnosed with an incurable illness, his second child got into some trouble and has to go to court, and his youngest child has a rare disease requiring surgery. On top of all of that, his wife's mother is suffering from stage four Cancer and has been given just weeks to live. While acknowledging that there are times when it is almost more than he can bear, he continues to demonstrate a remarkable faith and a joy that only God can give.

How do they do it, how do they keep going?

They have the promise of our Lord's presence to strengthen them in their darkest hour. Over and over they hear Him whisper to their spirit, "…surely I am with you always, to the very end of the age" (Matt. 28:20). "…Never will I leave you; never will I forsake you" (Heb. 13:5). As long as He is with them they can endure any hardship, bear any mistreatment or persecution, suffer any sickness or disease, because He will strengthen them. Like the Apostle Paul, they have learned to "…delight in weaknesses, in insults, in hardships, in persecutions, in difficulties…so that Christ's power may rest on (them)" (2 Cor. 12:10, 9).

They have learned to see with both eyes; to see not only the present tragedy but also the future triumph. Sometimes the future triumph is just around the corner. A young woman is instantly healed of an incurable bone disease, another woman receives a regenerative miracle when her dead thyroid is fully restored, a six-year-old boy is healed of Cancer, a pastor's blocked arteries are instantly opened making heart surgery unnecessary. Financial provision too—a struggling author receives several paying projects after praying for provision. A small congregation receives a one-time gift of $429,444.79 enabling them to finally move out of rented facilities where they have been holding services for ten years!

While supernatural interventions like these encourage our faith, they are no guarantee that God will do the same kind of thing for us. He may, but then again He may not. Faith is a factor, to be sure, but it is not the deciding factor. That's why Jesus taught us to pray for a miracle but to put our hope in God alone.

Jesus did not receive a supernatural deliverance in Gethsemane although He begged Father God to take the cup from Him. In fact the darkest time Jesus ever experienced was the final three hours of His earthly life. During that time He was utterly alone. God forsook Him! He bore what no believer will ever have to bear.

From the Father's perspective redemption's plan made perfect sense. Being a just God He could not forgive a single sinner until every sin—past, present, and future—was punished. Conversely, being a merciful God, He could not allow a single sinner to perish without making provision for their salvation.

So how could God be both just and merciful? The Cross was the answer—the only answer. When Jesus died on the Cross He suffered the full penalty for the sins of Adam's lost race, thus fully satisfying God's justice. Through His sacrificial death He also manifest the unconditional love of God, thus fully expressing God's mercy.

Seen from God's eternal perspective it was ingenious. Seen from our historical and biblical perspective it makes perfect sense. But from Jesus' earthly perspective it required an audacious act of faith. He "believed" He was laying down His life and He "believed" He could take it up again (see John 10:18), but He had no way of knowing for certain. What

He did on Golgotha was not only the greatest demonstration of love the world has ever seen but also its most daring act of faith! And even when God forsook Him, His faith never wavered. With His dying breath He screamed into the darkness, "Father [I still trust You] into your hands I commit my spirit" (Luke 23:46).

For those who loved Jesus, "Good Friday" was an unmitigated tragedy. When He died all their hopes and dreams died with Him. Friday night they were numb with grief, unable to comprehend the deadly turn of events. Saturday was no better. By Saturday night they were lost in a smothering fog of despair. From their earth bound perspective things couldn't get worse. But Father God saw things from a different perspective. He knew Sunday was coming. He knew that what appeared to be His waterloo was in fact His greatest victory. By dying Jesus made His entrance into the regions of the dead mandatory, and once He was there He proceeded to plunder them. He arose a victor from that dark domain and brought with Him the keys of death and hell! And by His death He destroyed him who held the power of death—the devil—and He freed those who were held in slavery by their fear of death. (See Heb. 2:14-15.)

Like those despairing disciples, you may be in a dark place. Your world may have come crashing down around you. Divorce may have ravished your family. Foreclosure may have taken your home and ruined you financially. Death may have taken your loved one. Don't give up! No matter how much you may have lost, no matter how dark it may seem, don't give up. Sunday's coming!

When you're in Gethsemane things can look hopeless. You know what I'm talking about. No matter how desperately you pray, things never seem to get any better. Worst of all it feels like God has forsaken you. The sense of His nearness that once sustained you seems to have vanished. You are left to wander alone in the darkness, stumbling over the wreckage of your world, or so it seems. But you are only seeing with one eye. For those who refuse to give up, who dare to see with both eyes, there's something beyond the darkness, something beyond the pain and brokenness of our shattered world. Whether God saves us from our "Gethsemane" or allows us to walk the "Via Dolorosa" (literally the sorrowful way) our ultimate deliverance is assured. "…He who believes in me," Jesus said, "will live, even though he dies" (John 11:25).

Sometimes Sunday is a long way off, maybe even in the next life, but knowing it's coming gives us the strength to live with joy no matter how difficult this present life.

> Therefore we do not lose heart. Though outwardly we are wasting away, yet inwardly we are being renewed day by day. For our light and

momentary troubles are achieving for us an eternal glory that far outweighs them all. So we fix our eyes not on what is seen, but on what is unseen. For what is seen is temporary, but what is unseen is eternal.

2 Corinthians 4:16-18

And like Jesus, we defy the darkness. "Father," we shout, "I still believe in You and into Your hands I commit my spirit!"

PRAYER

Lord Jesus, the tragedies of life can cause us to doubt your love and goodness; they can cause us to despair, to think You don't care about us. I reject those unscriptural thoughts. By an act of my will I choose to believe that You are truly touched by the feelings of my infirmities. You do see my situation. You do hear my desperate prayers. You do care about me and you are coming to my rescue. Help me to remain strong until You deliver me from all my troubles. In your holy name we pray. Amen.

Please read on for an excerpt from
Richard Exley's exciting novel

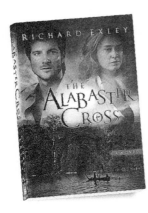

THE
ALABASTER
CROSS

PROLOGUE
AMAZON BASIN 1970

I watch as the old Indian makes his way across the
open area toward me. He is naked except for a loin-
cloth that is held in place by a leather string around
his waist. A lifetime of exposure to the sun has made
his dark skin coarse and left his face a web of wrin-
kles. In his hands he carries a stained canvas satchel.
The careful way in which he handles it makes me
know that it is valuable to him.

As he approaches I stand to my feet. He stops before me and speaks solemnly in a language I do not understand. The first thing I notice is the dark stains on the canvas, and then my eyes are drawn to a leather patch that is stitched to the flap between the buckles. Although the leather is old and stained, there is no mistaking the initials carved into it.

In an instant, I am taken back to a night more than twenty years ago. It is raining, and the drumming of the rain on the corrugated tin roof of the mission house is all too familiar. The rainy season is just beginning, and the thought of being trapped inside for weeks on end is nearly more than I can bear. My sister Helen, who is four years older than I am, is reading a book by the light of a kerosene lamp. Unlike me, she is an easygoing child. Nothing seems to bother her.

I am more like my father, who is intense and sometimes impatient. As far as he is concerned, life is serious business and must be lived with due sobriety. He comes from Puritan stock, and the generations that have separated him from his ancestors have done nothing to dilute their genes. Tonight he is muttering under his breath as he hastily stuffs supplies into packs for his trip into the interior. Already there are two large bundles beside the front door, and a third one is nearly finished.

The table is covered with supplies—rice, beans, coffee, smoked meat, bandages, medicine, and other medical supplies. My mother is helping him pack by checking things off of a long list as he stows them away. On more than one occasion, this careful attention to detail has meant the difference between life and death. In the jungles of the Amazon Basin a person seldom gets a second chance.

Although Father likes to pretend that these forays into the interior are routine, they are not. Danger lurks everywhere. Travel is treacherous, especially during the rainy season. In addition, there is the ever-present threat of accident or illness, not to mention the hostility of the Amuacas.

So why does he insist on going? Why does he risk leaving his wife a widow and his children without a father? There are at least two reasons for every trip. One is foundational, and it never changes. My father is nearly consumed with a desire to take the gospel to those who have never heard. As far as he is concerned, no risk is too great if he can but preach where no one has ever preached. The other reason varies with each trip, but it nearly always involves some kind of emergency.

Tomorrow's trip was occasioned when an Amuaca Indian stumbled into the mission compound more dead than alive. Using a combination of Portuguese and Indian dialects our indigenous workers were able to determine that his village had been stricken with a killing plague. Knowing that penicillin often opens the door for the preaching of the gospel, my father immediately began making preparations.

I listen as he carefully outlines the route he intends to take. It makes little sense to me, but my mother seems to understand. She is very supportive, but even I can tell that she is more than a little concerned.

According to my father, the stricken village is located four or five days upriver in an area previously unreached by any missionary. In response to my mother's concern he acknowledges that the trip will be grueling. Battling against the current of a rain-swollen river will be exhausting and make for slow going, not to mention the very real possibility of a flash flood now that the rainy season has set in. Still, it is the only way. Trying to go through the jungle on foot would be impossible.

Having carefully closed the third pack, my father sets it beside the other two near the front door. Putting on his spectacles, he draws the kerosene lamp close and reaches for his Bible. Without being asked, we all cease what we are doing and give him our attention. Following a prepared reading schedule, he turns to today's passage, Isaiah 43:1-3, and reads aloud:

> *But now thus saith the LORD that created thee, O Jacob, and he that formed thee, O Israel, Fear not: for I have redeemed thee, I have called thee by thy name; thou art mine. When thou passest through the waters, I will be with thee; and through the rivers, they shall not overflow thee: when thou walkest through the fire, thou shalt not be burned; neither shall the flame kindle upon thee. For I am the LORD thy God, the Holy One of Israel, thy Saviour.*

Although I am only seven years old and find much of the Bible hard to understand, even I cannot miss the significance of this passage given the present circumstances. Tears are glistening in my mother's eyes, and even my father looks pleased. Taking her hand, he says, "The Lord has spoken to us through His Word. No matter what dangers I may face, he will see me safely through."

After a brief prayer he bids my sister and me goodnight and sends us to bed. For some reason I cannot sleep, so I slip out of bed and make my way to the doorway that opens on the kitchen. A flimsy curtain serves as a door, and I pull it back the tiniest bit in order to peer out. My mother sits in a chair, her face in the shadows cast by the lamp. My father is moving about, gathering a few personal items for his trip. As I watch, I see him wrap his Bible and a leather-bound journal in an oilcloth and place them in his canvas satchel. Carefully he buckles the flap closed before reaching for my mother's hand …

To purchase a copy of Alabaster Cross
Order from your favorite bookstore
Or
Online at www.RichardExleyMinistries.org

MORE INSPIRING BOOKS FROM RICHARD EXLEY

YOU CAN JOURNEY BEYOND GRIEF AND LOSS TO FIND A PLACE OF PEACE, COMFORT AND HOPE...

For more than forty years author, Richard Exley, shared a special relationship with his father-in-law, a man he affectionately called Ben Roy. When he died Richard lost one of his dearest friends. Following his death, Richard found himself walking through the valley of the shadow of death, a journey he details with revealing candor in this book.

Although *From Grief to Gratefulness* is a deeply personal account of one family's grief, it is so much more. It is a story with a universal appeal. If you've ever lost a loved one you will find yourself identifying with the author as he explores the nuances of grief encountered in the weeks and month's following Ben's death and the impact they had on his life. Though consumed with memories of the way Ben died, he eventually allowed grief to do its healing work, and in time found himself remembering with a profound gratefulness the life Ben lived.

While honestly acknowledging the pain of losing a love one, *From Grief to Gratefulness* affirms the truth of Scripture and the promise of eternal life. Ultimately it will invite you to celebrate the precious gift of life.

**Order from your favorite bookstore
or visit the author's website
www.RichardExleyMinistries.org**

MORE INSPIRING BOOKS FROM RICHARD EXLEY

Do not despair! God is with you. That's the faith-affirming message of *Strength for the Storm*, a map for dealing with the troubles that inevitably arise in our lives.

Using dozens of real-life examples, contemporary and biblical, Richard Exley powerfully demonstrates how God not only guides us through difficult times but transforms those times into positive experiences for our ultimate good.

Whatever problems you face—illness, death, disaster, broken relationships, betrayal, financial difficulties—*Strength for the Storm* is filled with practical, Scripture-based lessons that will help you overcome.

Strength for the Storm is an invaluable reference for ministers, counselors, those enduring a crisis or tragedy, Christians who want to be prepared for future trials, and friends of anyone in the midst of trouble.

**Order from your favorite bookstore
or visit the author's website
www.RichardExleyMinistries.org**

MORE INSPIRING BOOKS FROM RICHARD EXLEY

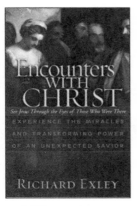

THIS IS YOUR PERSONAL INVITATION TO EXPERIENCE CHRIST IN A FRESH NEW WAY

Encounters with Christ is more than a book to be read. It is an opportunity to experience the transforming power of Jesus afresh in your own life.

Drawing from the canvases of Scripture, history, and tradition, Richard Exley carefully paints these real-life eyewitness accounts in colors so vivid you'll feel you're part of the story. Each vignette is filled with faith building insights that will strengthen and encourage you.

If you are ill, you will encounter the Healer. If you are being held back by fear or even in bondage to addiction, you will encounter the Once who can deliver the captive. If you are feeling overwhelmed or even discouraged, you will encounter the One whose presence will renew your faith and restore your joy.

Experience the wonder, compassion, and love of Christ through the personal accounts of those who encountered Him face-to-face. A Life Lesson that is perfect for personal reflection and small group discussion follows each vignette.

Order from your favorite bookstore
or visit the author's website
www.RichardExleyMinistries.org

www.RichardExleyMinistries.org